SEVEN WAYS OF THE CROSS

✠ ✠ ✠ ✠ ✠ ✠ ✠ ✠ ✠ ✠ ✠ ✠ ✠

Seven Ways of the Cross

⚜

BY JEAN GALOT, S.J.

*Translated by the Benedictine nuns
of Saint Cecilia's Abbey*

Angelico Press

✠ ✠ ✠ ✠ ✠ ✠ ✠ ✠

First published in the USA
by Angelico Press 2024

For information, address:
Angelico Press, Ltd.
169 Monitor St.
Brooklyn, NY 11222
www.angelicopress.com

ppr 979-8-89280-005-1
cloth 979-8-89280-006-8

Book and cover design
by Michael Schrauzer

It is not merely about
how much Jesus suffered,
but how much he loves.
Love transforms suffering into sacrifice....
That is love: the total gift of self.*

* Scott Hahn, foreword to Brant James Pitre, *Jesus and the Jewish Roots of the Eucharist: Unlocking the Secrets of the Last Supper* (New York: Doubleday, 2011), x.

CONTENTS

THIS WORK IS A NEW TRANSLA-tion by the Benedictine nuns of Saint Cecilia's Abbey, Ryde, Isle of Wight, United Kingdom, from an original French pamphlet printed in Louvain, Belgium, in 1958, and found in the library at the Abbey of Sainte-Marie des Deux-Montagnes, Canada.

Saint Cecilia's Abbey,
Ryde, Isle of Wight,
United Kingdom
MMXXIV

INTRODUCTION

THE WAY OF THE CROSS IS A devotion to the Sacred Passion of Our Lord Jesus in which we accompany Him in spirit on his sorrowful journey from the house of Pilate to Calvary. We recall with sorrow and love all that took place from his condemnation to his burial. The Way of the Cross is made up of 14 Stations, or stopping places. At each station we stop and ponder what happened there.

No special prayers are laid down, but it is customary to visit each station in order, reflecting devoutly on what is represented. This can be done anywhere mentally, or it can be prayerfully walked through by individuals or groups where physical Stations of the Cross have been set up, most often in churches. Public Stations of the Cross on Fridays in Lent is a popular practice in many parishes.

Meditating on Our Lord's Passion with the help of the Stations of the Cross is a fruitful practice in any season of the year.

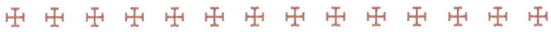

✠ ✠ ✠ ✠ ✠ ✠ ✠ ✠ ✠ ✠ ✠ ✠ ✠ ✠

1

⚜

A SHORT
WAY OF THE CROSS

✠ ✠ ✠ ✠ ✠ ✠ ✠ ✠

I

✠

JESUS IS CONDEMNED TO DEATH

Jesus, our Savior,

It is done. You are condemned to death for us. Your judges do not take your life from you; it is you who give it to the Heavenly Father, freely and willingly. Did you not come into this world to offer yourself as a sacrifice?

Enable us to understand that our life, associated with yours, is also destined for sacrifice; enable us to give up our human dreams of a pleasant and easy existence. Give us the strength to offer willingly the sacrifices that are required of us, and to walk our way of the cross with you to the end.

⚜

II

✠

JESUS RECEIVES HIS CROSS

Jesus, our Savior,

When they loaded the Cross on your already bruised shoulders, you took it with much love, because in this Cross, which came to aggravate your pains, you recognized the burden which the Heavenly Father intended for you; and you welcomed it generously so that we might do the same.

Enable us to take up our cross every day without complaint, as a gift sent by the Father; enable us to carry it with great love, happy to have something we can offer to God!

⚜

III

✠

JESUS FALLS
THE FIRST TIME

Jesus, our Savior,

Your first fall puts our own falls before our eyes: you fall on the road to your torment because you are carrying the weight of so many moral falls. But immediately you get up again, to give us the strength to get up in our turn.

When we have offended God, give us the humility to recognize our weakness and the courage to start out again more resolutely. Heal our deep misery by purifying our souls and renewing our love for you.

⚜

IV

✠

JESUS MEETS
HIS MOTHER

Jesus, our Savior,

Enable us to participate intimately in your meeting with Mary. What an exchange of looks, revealing a common desire to suffer and to offer oneself! What resolve to accomplish the Father's will together!

So that we can unite ourselves more firmly to this resolve, may our Heavenly Mother's gaze come to meet us as we tread our path, especially when our crosses seem to be heavy. May her generous gaze encourage us to endure everything more willingly and to follow you unfailingly along the path of sacrifice!

⚜

V

✠

SIMON HELPS JESUS TO CARRY HIS CROSS

Jesus, our Savior,

You did not want to carry your Cross alone. You wanted to share it with us as love is shared.

Apparently, we are requisitioned, forced to "take up the cross," like Simon of Cyrene. But may we understand the honor that you do us in uniting us with your lot, the kindness that you show us by asking us to carry a cross with you when you are always carrying the heaviest part of it! May we thank you for wanting to unite our suffering so closely with yours!

⚜

VI

✠

VERONICA WIPES
THE FACE OF JESUS

Jesus, our Savior,

It is no longer to Veronica, it is to us that you show your face so that we can contemplate and love it. Stimulate our fervor to seek to meet your gaze, to recognize and know you.

And since you no longer want to imprint your sorrowful face on a cloth but on our souls, communicate your generosity to us, enabling us to accept everything and to give all. Make our hearts an image of yours, by deeply engraving in it a love capable of the greatest sacrifices!

⚜

VII

✠

JESUS FALLS
THE SECOND TIME

Jesus, our Savior,

Your second fall provokes the mockery and contempt of your enemies; you seem so weak to them, so overwhelmed, and they do not understand that you are content with this utter weakness which is part of your offering.

Help us, like you, to offer our weakness to God, and not to rebel in the face of contempt or humiliation. Instead of seeking the first place, make us ready to accept the last place, and to sacrifice our self-esteem in order to be more like you.

⚜

VIII

☩

JESUS SPEAKS TO THE WOMEN OF JERUSALEM

Jesus, our Savior,

In the midst of great suffering, you think of others rather than of yourself. You are more concerned about the future sorrows of the women of Jerusalem than about your present torment.

Share with us this nobility of soul which will prevent us from turning in on ourselves when pain or trials arise, and which will incline us to be more considerate of our neighbors, to sympathize with them, to console them, and to strengthen them in generous forgetfulness of our own difficulties.

⚜

IX

✠

JESUS FALLS
THE THIRD TIME

Jesus, our Savior,

You fall for the third time, but you get up again and continue on your path, despite your exhaustion.

Through this perseverance, teach us never to give in to weariness or discouragement. May our falls never serve as a pretext for giving up the struggle, nor our weaknesses as a reason to stop on the way! Help us overcome the temptation to give up, by leaning more firmly on your unwavering courage. At each obstacle, stimulate us anew to go forward!

⚜

X

✝

JESUS IS STRIPPED OF HIS GARMENTS

Jesus, our Savior,

You allow yourself to be stripped of everything, in order to die in the most absolute poverty.

Cut the chains that bind us to the goods of this world, and show us the vanity of those goods, which will not follow us in the hereafter. Make us really poor in spirit, so that we may be freer to love you, and more aware of receiving everything from God. Be henceforward our only good, the one for which we are ready to abandon everything else!

⚜

XI

✠

JESUS IS NAILED TO THE CROSS

Jesus, our Savior,

The terrible blows that drive the nails into your hands and feet tear no cry or complaint out of you.

How we need this sight to find in it a support for our patience! By your example, teach us to endure everything calmly and without irritation, to be silent even when we judge our situation intolerable. Inspire in us your gentleness as the only response to violence and injustice. Whenever we might be tempted to seek revenge, maintain charity within us!

⚜

XII

✠

JESUS DIES
ON THE CROSS

Jesus, our Savior,

It is in deep distress of soul that you consummate your sacrifice, for you have the impression of being abandoned by your Father. But with an even deeper confidence, you surrender yourself into his hands and hand your life over to Him.

In times of darkness, depression, or inner emptiness, give us the strength to stand firm, consummating our sacrifice and offering our distress to God. Above all, fill us with an attitude of complete surrender to the will of our Heavenly Father!

⚜

XIII

✠

JESUS IS TAKEN DOWN FROM THE CROSS

Jesus, our Savior,

Your body is taken down from the Cross and handed over to your Mother for a few moments. With what sorrowful devotion does Mary accept this precious burden!

Your body is also entrusted to us, but this time full of life: through Holy Communion, it is given to us entirely. May your Mother help us to make this Communion a moment of true devotion, when we fervently receive you and your love, and can be filled with your life and your victorious strength!

⚜

XIV

✠

JESUS IS LAID
IN THE TOMB

Jesus, our Savior,

The stone closed over your tomb and everything seemed finished. And yet, it is in this tomb that the triumph will take place, on the morning of your Resurrection.

Enable us to understand that sacrifice is fruitful, and that suffering, generously offered, inevitably turns into joy. By uniting ourselves with the humility of your self-surrender and your self-sacrificing love, may we persevere in faith and hope! Lord, placed in the tomb, be for us the guarantee of the final happiness which will crown sacrifice!

⚜

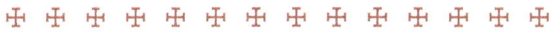

✠ ✠ ✠ ✠ ✠ ✠ ✠ ✠ ✠ ✠ ✠ ✠ ✠

2

⚜

A MARIAN
WAY OF THE CROSS

✠ ✠ ✠ ✠ ✠ ✠ ✠ ✠

I

✠

JESUS IS CONDEMNED TO DEATH

Generous Mother,

When you heard the death sentence fall from Pilate's lips, you said "yes" to the divine will, which made use of human authority to demand a terrible sacrifice from you.

Help us to say our "yes" unhesitatingly whenever a sacrifice is asked of us, by recognizing in the events or in the men who impose a sacrifice on us an expression of the Heavenly Father's will.

"Yes, Father, here I am, entirely yours."

⚜

II

✠

JESUS RECEIVES HIS CROSS

Generous Mother,

If it had been possible, you would have carried the Cross yourself, to take all the shame and pain on your shoulders.

But since your Son wanted to carry it, you wished at least to unite your heart with his sufferings.

By inspiring in us a greater love for Christ, make us eager to unite our hearts with his self-offering; strengthen in us a desire to share willingly in his abasement and his sorrow.

⚜

III

✠

JESUS FALLS
THE FIRST TIME

Generous Mother,

You saw Jesus fall to the ground, and you knew that by doing this He wanted to save men from their moral misery. By this fall, He makes it possible for us to get up again.

Help us to make use of the strength our Savior gives to us, and to want to live in great purity.

You, who have never fallen into sin and who have always preserved your holiness immaculate, share with us your care to avoid the slightest faults for the sake of Christ.

⚜

IV

✠

JESUS MEETS HIS MOTHER

Generous Mother,

You wanted to follow your Son as closely as possible, to be with Him throughout this painful path, for you wanted your soul to be in harmony with His, to offer Him all your sympathy and complete solidarity in his sufferings.

Be there also on our way of the cross, very close to us, when trials overwhelm us or when the hour of sacrifice strikes.

Be there to comfort us, and may your maternal sympathy encourage us to go forward and not faint!

Be there to shed the light of your gentle smile on our sorrowful path!

⚜

V

✠

SIMON HELPS JESUS TO CARRY HIS CROSS

Generous Mother,

How you would have wished to be in that place imposed on Simon of Cyrene, close to Jesus beneath the Cross! And how you suddenly loved the stranger, to whom this special place had just been granted!

When this lot falls to us too, show us all the love we can have for our Savior in it, all the intimacy we can find there with Him.

Help us not to complain; help us to rejoice in being able to carry the Cross with Jesus. Help us, above all, to be aware there of your loving gaze upon us!

⚜

VI

✠

VERONICA WIPES
THE FACE OF JESUS

Generous Mother,

The face of Jesus had long been imprinted within you far more deeply than in Veronica's veil. You had this face in your soul, for you had contemplated it ceaselessly for many years.

Now, on the road to Calvary the features of your Son, disfigured by mistreatment, are imprinted on you again and you recognize there love taken to its climax.

Teach us how to look at Christ, how to discover the depth of His love in the sorrowful face of the Crucified One.

⚜

VII

✠

JESUS FALLS
THE SECOND TIME

Generous Mother,

The second fall of Jesus brought home, before
your very eyes, the merciless cruelty of His
adversaries. But you responded with a benevo-
lence which excused and forgave the wickedness
raining down upon your Son who is so good.
Your gentleness remained unshaken; you refused
to be angry.

When we are offended or oppressed, and
are tempted to blame the wickedness of others,
enable us to respond with gentleness, promptly
forgetting what has hurt us and forgiving completely and definitively.

❧

VIII

✝

JESUS SPEAKS TO THE WOMEN OF JERUSALEM

Generous Mother,

As you heard Jesus predict the calamities that would fall upon the people of Jerusalem, you shared His compassion. No misery leaves you unconcerned.

You have always been attentive to the sufferings of others, and with a mother's love you embrace all our human distress.

Be for us the Mother of mercy; be our refuge in misfortune and in weakness, the refuge where we are sure to find understanding and compassion. The greater our pain, the more completely we trust in you!

⚜

IX

✠

JESUS FALLS
THE THIRD TIME

Generous Mother,

The third fall was another blow to your maternal heart. Although it was more painful than the previous ones, you did not protest or complain that God was demanding too much of you, or that the sacrifice was too cruel.

You put no limit on your generosity and, seeing your Son valiantly getting up again, you promised to follow Him to the end.

Share this generous attitude with us, so that we may never find the trial sent to us excessive and that we may accept it with magnanimous and persevering hearts.

⚜

X

☩

JESUS IS STRIPPED OF HIS GARMENTS

Generous Mother,

Seeing your Son stripped of His garments strengthened you in your resolve to accept all the renunciations willed by our Heavenly Father.

You even surrendered yourself to the supreme sacrifice of losing your only child.

When the Heavenly Father asks us to make a sacrifice that costs us a great deal, help us not to shrink from offering it to Him. Enable us to give lovingly all that God wants to take from us!

⚜

XI

☩

JESUS IS NAILED TO THE CROSS

Generous Mother,

As the nails pierced the hands and feet of your Son, you united your silence with His. These are the hands that you used to hold so often, and the feet that you taught to walk. The blows hammered upon your own heart, but not a word escaped your lips.

Teach us to remain silent in our sorrows, in the bruises inflicted on us. Teach us the heroic silence which conceals and consummates our interior sacrifice!

⚜

XII

✠

JESUS DIES ON THE CROSS

Generous Mother,

Before expiring, Jesus, indicating the beloved disciple, addressed you: "Woman, behold, your son" (Jn 19:26). Thus, you became the Mother of each one of the Master's beloved disciples, the Mother of us all.

Thank you, O Mary, for accepting this new maternal mission! It is such a beautiful fruit of the Savior's sacrifice and of your own sacrifice!

Following the example of Saint John, we too would like to take you into our homes, to welcome you into our lives with filial hearts, to love you, and to help those around us love you as the Mother of us all!

⚜

XIII

✠

JESUS IS TAKEN DOWN FROM THE CROSS

Generous Mother,

When you received the inanimate body of Jesus in your arms, your sorrow reached its summit. How heart-breaking it was to contemplate that face, whose marvelous animation you had admired so many times, lifeless now!

At that moment, you surrendered yourself once more to the divine will, and you offered your sorrow with more love than ever for the souls to be saved.

Enable us to see the Father's will and the good of souls in our sacrifices!

⚜

XIV

✠

JESUS IS LAID
IN THE TOMB

Generous Mother,

When you left the tomb where the body of
Jesus had just been placed, you did not give up
hope. You remembered that your Son had fore-
told His Resurrection, and this thought filled
you with confidence.

When we are tempted to let ourselves be discouraged, show us the path to hope; remind us
how your hope on Good Friday, the day when
all seemed lost, received infallible confirmation
in the triumph of Easter Sunday!

⚜

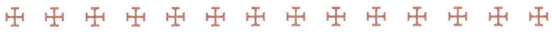

✝ ✝ ✝ ✝ ✝ ✝ ✝ ✝ ✝ ✝ ✝ ✝ ✝ ✝

3

⚜

A CONTEMPLATIVE
WAY OF THE CROSS

✝ ✝ ✝ ✝ ✝ ✝ ✝ ✝

I

✠

JESUS IS CONDEMNED TO DEATH

Loving Lord,

Let us contemplate the love that prompted you to offer yourself as a sacrifice. This is the long-awaited hour when you will give us the utmost proof of your love. "Greater love has no man than this, that a man lay down his life for his friends" (Jn 15:13). In the death sentence, you see only one thing: the opportunity to give yourself completely.

Thank you, O Lord, for the supreme gift of your love when you offered yourself to the torments of Calvary for us!

⚜

II

✠

JESUS RECEIVES HIS CROSS

Loving Lord,

The Cross is placed on your shoulders. It is very heavy — especially after the pain and wounds of the scourging — but in your burning desire to give and to sacrifice yourself, it is light. You receive it zealously, and you want it to be forever the symbol of your love for men.

Thank you, Lord, for the ardent love which made you welcome the Cross with joy and carry it with courage!

⚜

III

✠

JESUS FALLS
THE FIRST TIME

Loving Lord,

The fall that you cannot avoid shows us that
you wanted to give us all your strength. There
is nothing you do not want to sacrifice for our
salvation and our happiness. When you fall, your
love neither fails nor falters; on the contrary, it
is strengthened in your will to walk all the way
to Calvary.

Thank you, Lord, for the inexhaustible love
with which you spent yourself for us completely!

⚜

IV

✠

JESUS MEETS
HIS MOTHER

Loving Lord,

Here you are in the presence of your Mother. In this moving meeting of two sorrows, we see the meeting of two loves moving in the same direction and wanting to walk side by side. You inspired in Mary a love of souls like your own love for them, and you encouraged her to give everything for us as you do yourself.

Thank you, Lord, for having united to your love the love of a Mother who sacrifices herself for her countless children!

⚜

V

✠

SIMON HELPS JESUS TO CARRY HIS CROSS

Loving Lord,

How encouragingly you looked at Simon of Cyrene when the soldiers forced him to carry the Cross with you! You have such a great desire to entrust part of your Cross to us, for it is with our collaboration that you want to effect the redemption of humanity! There is so much love in the opportunity given to Simon!

Thank you, Lord, for the love you show us every time you ask us to carry your redemptive Cross with you!

⚜

VI

☩

VERONICA WIPES
THE FACE OF JESUS

Loving Lord,

Like Veronica, may we carry away with us
the unforgettable memory of your sorrowful
face! Help us to understand all the love that is
expressed in the face of our Savior and engrave
your image forever in our minds. May your loving face remain constantly present before our
eyes, and may it be our comfort in the difficult
moments of our existence!

Thank you, Lord, for having left us the image
of a God who suffers for love!

⚜

VII

✠

JESUS FALLS
THE SECOND TIME

Loving Lord,

In your second fall, it is your humility that speaks to us. You hide your heroism under such wretched appearances! You did not want to make your way of the Cross a proud and triumphant path; you wanted to suffer humbly, like any one of us, with all our human weaknesses!

Thank you, Lord, for being made like us out of love for us, and for having fallen in order to make yourself lower than us!

⚜

VIII

✠

JESUS SPEAKS TO THE WOMEN OF JERUSALEM

Loving Lord,

You can think of others, even when you are suffering so much! Your words of sympathy to the women of Jerusalem show the extent of your love: your heart does not contract in your suffering but expands, filled with compassion for the future trials of humanity. You prove that from now on you want to be with all those who suffer.

Thank you, Lord, for the great consolation you give us by sympathizing so profoundly with all our sufferings!

⚜

IX

✠

JESUS FALLS
THE THIRD TIME

Loving Lord,

Allow us to admire in your third fall the invincible courage which, despite increasingly overwhelming pain, brings you to your feet once more and makes you take to the road again. Your love is tireless and overcomes all obstacles. The more the difficulties grow, the more your will to save us responds with generosity and perseverance.

Thank you, Lord, for giving us the assurance of your absolutely faithful love which is stronger than all our human weaknesses!

⚜

X

✠

JESUS IS STRIPPED OF HIS GARMENTS

Loving Lord,

When you are stripped of your clothes, you are happy to give all you have left. You already had so little, you who had nowhere to lay your head; now you have nothing left at all, showing us the truth of the beatitude you taught us. What joy it is for you to be poor without limit!

Thank you, Lord, for the overflowing fullness of love that radiates from your nakedness!

⚜

XI

✠

JESUS IS NAILED
TO THE CROSS

Loving Lord,

Your enemies want to nail you once and for all to the Cross but you have an even greater desire to be attached to it, for it is from the Cross that you will draw all men to yourself. You want to be inseparable from this Cross, just as you are inseparable from your love. Enable us to be attracted toward this Cross, wherein we shall find hidden the ardor of your burning love!

Thank you, Lord, for having welcomed the nails into your wounded body, so that the Cross might everywhere proclaim the greatness of your love!

⚜

XII

☩

JESUS DIES
ON THE CROSS

Loving Lord,

Your love for the Heavenly Father is consummated at the moment when you abandon your soul into His hands. At the same moment, your love for men reaches its most sublime intensity, and is expressed mysteriously in the painful cry: "I thirst" (Jn 19:28). You who loved us so much, you thirst for a love that will answer yours!

Thank you, Lord, for giving us your last breath, and for thirsting for us!

⚜

XIII

✠

JESUS IS TAKEN DOWN FROM THE CROSS

Loving Lord,

In your lifeless body, taken down from the Cross, your love still speaks. The gaping wound in your side makes us realize that you have spared yourself absolutely nothing, that you have kept nothing at all for yourself. The pallor of your face reminds us that your blood has been shed freely and completely. And you leave your body here below, yielding it entirely to men.

Thank you, Lord, for abandoning yourself again to us from the height of the Cross after having offered your life for us!

⚜

XIV

✠

JESUS IS LAID IN THE TOMB

Loving Lord,

You are disappearing into the darkness of the tomb, but your love remains, even if your body is hidden from our eyes. And this love assures us of your triumph. Nothing and no one will be able to prevent you from coming out of the sepulcher, or prevent your love, hidden for now in the dark, from undertaking the conquest of the world!

Thank you, Lord, for storing up so much hidden love, in order to pour it out on us all the more abundantly!

❧

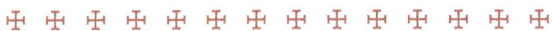

✠ ✠ ✠ ✠ ✠ ✠ ✠ ✠ ✠ ✠ ✠ ✠ ✠

4

⚜

A REPARATORY
WAY OF THE CROSS

✠ ✠ ✠ ✠ ✠ ✠ ✠ ✠

I

✠

JESUS IS CONDEMNED TO DEATH

Jesus, offered as a victim,

You submit to the death sentence because you want to make reparation, through the total homage of your life to the Heavenly Father, for the outrages committed against Him by our sins.

By guiding us along the way of the cross, unite us to your intention of making reparation. Help us to render to the Father the total homage of ourselves in reparation for the sins of the world!

⚜

II

✠

JESUS RECEIVES HIS CROSS

Jesus, offered as a victim,

It is with a surge of love that you take up your Cross for you wish to compensate, with your absolute generosity for all, our lack of love toward our Heavenly Father.

Help us also to accept our sufferings with a generous outpouring of love, in reparation for so much cowardice on our part and that of others!

⚜

III

✠

JESUS FALLS
THE FIRST TIME

Jesus, offered as a victim,

In your fall, it is the crushing burden of the sins of the world that brings you to the ground; you are making up for the heavy propensity toward evil which plunges humanity down so low.

Give us the strength to resist all the snares of sin, and to make up for our falls by having the courage to overcome temptation!

⚜

IV

✠

JESUS MEETS HIS MOTHER

Jesus, offered as a victim,

From the midst of the sinful world which surrounds you on all sides your Mother, the only immaculate creature, comes to you. Holy and innocent she offers, like you, her pure heart in reparation for the sins of others.

Sinful though we are, inspire us to unite our offerings with Mary's perfectly holy oblation so that the reparation we offer may have more value in the Father's eyes.

⚜

V

✠

SIMON HELPS JESUS
TO CARRY HIS CROSS

Jesus, offered as a victim,

You judged Simon of Cyrene worthy of sharing the burden of offering reparation for the sins of the world. What a privilege you bestow on him in taking him as a collaborator in your sacrifice!

Enable us to understand the privilege you grant us when you send us suffering, thus allowing us to collaborate with you in your great work of reparation!

⚜

VI

✠

VERONICA WIPES
THE FACE OF JESUS

Jesus, offered as a victim,

If you leave Veronica with an image of your face it is not just so that we might lovingly contemplate your sorrowful features but also that we may be willing to conform our conduct to yours.

Show us how our faces can be like yours, if we welcome and gladly offer our trials as a precious occasion of reparation for so many sins!

⚜

VII

✞

JESUS FALLS
THE SECOND TIME

Jesus, offered as a victim,

By your second fall, you consent to appearing small and weak. It is in this way that you redeem our immense human pride — hungry for greatness and power — the profound root of sin.

Impregnate us with your humility, with your joy in welcoming humiliations, in reparation for our frequent outbursts of pride!

⚜

VIII

✠

JESUS SPEAKS TO THE WOMEN OF JERUSALEM

Jesus, offered as a victim,

In your response to the expressions of sympathy from the women of Jerusalem, you give us to understand that we should pity not those who offer themselves for the redemption of their brethren, but those who persevere in their sins.

So that obstinate sinners may receive the grace they so urgently need to return to you, we offer ourselves in union with you for the redemption of their souls!

⚜

IX

✠

JESUS FALLS
THE THIRD TIME

Jesus, offered as a victim,

By your courage in getting up again from your
third fall, you redeem our far too frequent dis-
couragements, failures, desertions, apostasies,
and acts of despair.

Maintain our courageous fidelity, so that we
can contribute to the amending of infidelities
and help to lift up broken spirits!

⚜

X

JESUS IS STRIPPED OF HIS GARMENTS

Jesus, offered as a victim,

By letting yourself be stripped of your garments, you offer yourself in reparation for all attachment to wealth, and greed for money, as well as for impurity, lack of modesty, and the lusts of the flesh.

By a spirit detached from the goods of this world, make us repair so much ferocious greed and, by our purity of heart, so much miserable degradation!

⚜

XI

✠

JESUS IS NAILED
TO THE CROSS

Jesus, offered as a victim,

As the nails pierce your flesh you give us one
last image of your gentle and humble heart. With
your silence and your gentleness, you redeem our
violence, our impatience, and our anger.

Enable us to share in your meekness and,
in all our difficulties, grant us the strength of
unshakeable patience in union with your redemptive patience!

⚜

XII

✠

JESUS DIES
ON THE CROSS

Jesus, offered as a victim,

Shortly before rendering your last breath to the Father, you implore Him on behalf of your enemies. This forgiveness granted to such cruel adversaries is a cry of love which redeems so much vengeance and enmity!

Enable us to meet all the demands of love of neighbor, and strengthen our courage to forgive immediately so as to repair so much hatred and bitterness!

⚜

XIII

✠

JESUS IS TAKEN DOWN FROM THE CROSS

Jesus, offered as a victim,

When Mary receives your body taken down from the Cross, she completes in her heart what is still lacking for her compassion to be fully consummated: a sword pierces her soul, as the lance has just pierced your side.

Stir up in us a generosity like hers so that we too can continue to the end the work of redemption and reparation!

⚜

XIV

✠

JESUS IS LAID
IN THE TOMB

Jesus, offered as a victim,

Your body being placed in the tomb shows that you have given your all, in order to redeem those whom sin had condemned to the death of the soul. You enter the sepulcher so that we may be worthy to leave it.

Help us to die to ourselves so as to receive the wonderful fruit of your superabundant reparation: your triumphant divine life!

⚜

✠ ✠ ✠ ✠ ✠ ✠ ✠ ✠ ✠ ✠ ✠ ✠ ✠ ✠

5

⚜

AN APOSTOLIC
WAY OF THE CROSS

✠ ✠ ✠ ✠ ✠ ✠ ✠ ✠

I

✠

JESUS IS CONDEMNED
TO DEATH

Jesus, our liberator,

You came to this earth precisely for the hour of the Passion, for this death sentence, because you had only one objective: to free our souls through your sacrifice.

Give us the apostolic zeal which is ready to sacrifice everything, to offer everything, for the salvation of souls.

May the thought of souls to be saved guide and sustain us in our activities and in our sacrifices!

⚜

II

✠

JESUS RECEIVES HIS CROSS

Jesus, our liberator,

The weight of the Cross is very heavy on your shoulders, but it seems lighter to you because it is your love of souls that bears the weight.

Inspire me with this same love, which will make me bear my sorrows and my difficulties more cheerfully, in the joy of being able to offer them for the salvation of others.

By enabling me to accept pain, may you foster in me genuine apostolic zeal!

⚜

III

✠

JESUS FALLS
THE FIRST TIME

Jesus, our liberator,

By your fall, you obtain for souls fallen into sin the strength to free themselves from it.

Make me think more often about the plight of those who have become slaves to their passions and who need great courage to break those bonds and straighten out their lives.

May I be prepared to accept the humiliations associated with your fall in order to obtain this courage for them!

⚜

IV

✠

JESUS MEETS HIS MOTHER

Jesus, our liberator,

Mary completely shared your ideal and, like you, she thought about the great work to be done: the salvation of all humanity. That is why she wanted to suffer with you.

I would like to imitate her, to pursue this lofty goal in my life, and to collaborate with you in its realization. May this great apostolic intention underpin my life and make me more generous, more ready for sacrifice!

⚜

V

✠

SIMON HELPS JESUS TO CARRY HIS CROSS

Jesus, our liberator,

You willed to need Simon of Cyrene to carry your Cross to Calvary. You want to need each one of us to complete your work of redemption.

Since you give us this honor and this trust, and the salvation of our brothers depends on us, may we want to devote our strength to helping souls and doing them good.

⚜

VI

✠

VERONICA WIPES THE FACE OF JESUS

Jesus, our liberator,

When Veronica receives the image of your face it is radiant with sweetness and love. You want to achieve victory over your opponents through kindness.

In the spiritual battle in which we are engaged, help us to understand the importance of kindness, teach us to show sympathy and love to everyone, even those who seem to be hostile, and enable us to use only the weapon of charity.

⚜

VII

✠

JESUS FALLS
THE SECOND TIME

Jesus, our liberator,

By your second fall, convince us that our weaknesses and misery can contribute to the good of souls, if we offer them to God with humility.

They lead us to let go of all human support and to put all our trust in God's power. Only your power can save and sanctify souls, and you do this precisely through our incapacity. Use our powerlessness for your apostolic work!

⚜

VIII

✠

JESUS SPEAKS TO THE WOMEN OF JERUSALEM

Jesus, our liberator,

By carrying your Cross, you help us to carry ours. By your words of sympathy to the women of Jerusalem, you strove to lift up their souls, to enable them to endure their trials.

Grant that in comforting others, we may always have this apostolic concern of lifting up their souls, giving them enough strength to carry their crosses nobly!

⚜

IX

✠

JESUS FALLS
THE THIRD TIME

Jesus, our liberator,

May your third fall teach us never to be discouraged in our apostolic zeal!

If we meet resistance or experience setbacks, help us not to give up the fight.

Since your grace precedes us, help us to persevere in our efforts relentlessly and to do everything we can for the salvation of a soul!

⚜

X

✠

JESUS IS STRIPPED OF HIS GARMENTS

Jesus, our liberator,

You allow yourself to be stripped of the little you have left, for you want to give men everything.

Stir up in us the desire to give everything, and to welcome every renunciation, so that other souls can be enriched with graces.

When a sacrifice is required of us, enable us not to consider what it costs us, but rather how much value it can have for our neighbor!

⚜

XI

✠

JESUS IS NAILED
TO THE CROSS

Jesus, our liberator,

You allow your flesh to be crucified so that men can overcome the passions of their flesh.

Thank you for consenting to such a sacrifice in order to enable us to lead pure lives, in spite of all the temptations that may assail us.

Enable me, by my purity, to help other souls to free themselves from their slavery to carnal pleasures and to seek the true joy of your love!

⚜

XII

✠

JESUS DIES
ON THE CROSS

Jesus, our liberator,

On the Cross, you thirst. And you want to share this great thirst for souls with us.

Help us to understand better the value of a single soul, since you wanted to save us by paying the price of your life for each and every one of us.

May we foster this burning desire within us, and may we quench your thirst by bringing souls to you through our sacrifices!

⚜

XIII

✠

JESUS IS TAKEN DOWN FROM THE CROSS

Jesus, our liberator,

It is consummated. Your body is handed over to your holy Mother. Mary accepts losing you and henceforth regards us as her children.

May her maternal care for souls nourish our apostolic confidence!

By giving Mary as Mother to each of us, you facilitated our salvation and you invite us to carry out our apostolate in close union with her.

⚜

XIV

✠

JESUS IS LAID IN THE TOMB

Jesus, our liberator,

Placing your body in the tomb seems to be burying the fruit of your sacrifice. And yet this fruit remains, although it is hidden, and it is immense: humanity is saved.

Give us confidence in the effectiveness of the sacrifices we make for the good of souls. The fruits remain hidden, but we have to believe in them. Instill this consoling truth into us: the humble sacrifice, unknown to all, bears tremendous invisible fruit.

⚜

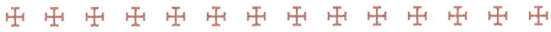

✠ ✠ ✠ ✠ ✠ ✠ ✠ ✠ ✠ ✠ ✠ ✠ ✠

6

⚜

AN ECCLESIAL
WAY OF THE CROSS

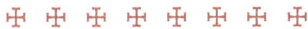

✠ ✠ ✠ ✠ ✠ ✠ ✠ ✠

I

⊞

JESUS IS CONDEMNED
TO DEATH

O good Shepherd,

By accepting your death sentence, you decide the future of your disciples, who will also be drawn to total sacrifice. It is the whole Church that you commit to the way of the cross. Since her fate is linked to yours, and her mission continues yours, it is through suffering that she must open to men the path of salvation.

Help us to participate with all our heart in your entire Church's way of the cross!

⚜

II

✠

JESUS RECEIVES HIS CROSS

O good Shepherd,

The weight of the Cross, which falls so heavily on your shoulders, is the weight of the Church that you want to lift and raise up to great holiness. We are all sinners whose debt you want to pay, transforming us into pure, new souls, and giving us a new inclination toward the good. By taking up the Cross, you assure the Church of victory over evil.

Help us to accept fully within ourselves the innocence and purity to which you want to raise your Church!

⚜

III

✠

JESUS FALLS
THE FIRST TIME

O good Shepherd,

Your fall shows us the divine power which manifests itself in human weakness. It is through this weakness that you are going to triumph. It will be the same for your Church, whose journey is to be hindered by many weaknesses without, however, ceasing to progress thanks to the irresistible energy with which you endow her. You want her to be humanly fragile in order to make her divinely powerful.

Help us to believe in the victorious destiny of the Church, despite all the weaknesses we may witness!

⚜

IV

✠

JESUS MEETS HIS MOTHER

O good Shepherd,

Among the crowd around you one face stands out, that of your Mother. She is the perfect example of a soul unreservedly united with your sacrifice. Mary fulfils the task the Church is going to have of being one with your suffering love. In your Mother, who becomes the Mother of all men, you meet the Church herself in her most admirable symbol.

Help us to follow in Mary's footsteps, the better to meet you, and the more closely to unite ourselves, along with the whole Church, to your sacrifice!

❧

V

✠

SIMON HELPS JESUS TO CARRY HIS CROSS

O good Shepherd,

By having yourself assisted by Simon of Cyrene, you reveal how much you long for us all to be companions on your path to Calvary. It is through suffering and trials that you want us to enter into intimacy with you. So it is that the Church is closest to you in her suffering members; it is through the Cross that you want to make her enter most deeply into your love.

Help us to draw closer to you and to your heart in moments of suffering!

⚜

VI

✠

VERONICA WIPES
THE FACE OF JESUS

O good Shepherd,

It is to the Church that you have left the memory of your face as our Redeemer. Even more so than in a cloth, your features are imprinted in the Gospels, of which the Church is the guardian and the interpreter. It is she who tells us about you and your saving love; it is through her that you want to convey to us the true image of your face.

Help us to remain faithful to the Church, to recognize you more and more in your true face.

⚜

VII

✠

JESUS FALLS
THE SECOND TIME

O good Shepherd,

Your second fall seems a humiliation in the eyes of all and provides your enemies with an opportunity for fresh mockery and outrage. You did not want a glorious procession for your Church, for she is to be far removed from the world's pride. You assign her a destiny where humiliations and derision play a redemptive role.

Help us to enter sincerely into the Church's spirit of humility, and not to be ashamed of her when her adversaries mock her!

⚜

VIII

✠

JESUS SPEAKS TO THE WOMEN OF JERUSALEM

O good Shepherd,

As you console the women of Jerusalem, it is the misfortune of a whole people that you deplore. Your gaze extends to all those who resist your call, to all who refuse to join your Church. You are filled with compassion for their inner misery, and it is for their greater happiness that you wish to see them finally enter into your one fold.

Help us to bear witness to your love to those who do not yet belong to your Mystical Body!

⚜

IX

✠

JESUS FALLS
THE THIRD TIME

O good Shepherd,

Your third fall further highlights the indomitable courage with which you continue along the road despite your exhaustion. It foretells your Church's courage when she will be overwhelmed by her persecutors and apparently suffer serious failures, but will be tireless in her perseverance. It is through persecutions and setbacks that you want to lead her to her triumph.

Help us to stand firm in the storms that assail the Church, and may you preserve the fidelity of persecuted Christians!

⚜

X

✠

JESUS IS STRIPPED OF HIS GARMENTS

O good Shepherd,

After living in poverty, you want to die in total nakedness. It is for the Church to continue here below your exemplary life of poverty, and the generosity of your self-denial. Just as you have heaped your spiritual riches upon the Church, so also you want her to be entirely detached from the goods of this world.

Help us to be detached from earthly goods, and foster within us a spirit of poverty, generosity, and unselfishness!

⚜

XI

✠

JESUS IS NAILED
TO THE CROSS

O good Shepherd,

By the nails that dig into your hands and feet, you are the model of those in your Church who endure great bodily suffering. You have sanctified these sufferings and made them an instrument of redemption; that is why you send them to the members of your Church, along with the strength to endure them patiently.

Help us to recognize in all our sorrows the price for the salvation of souls and the means of extending your Kingdom!

⚜

XII

✠

JESUS DIES
ON THE CROSS

O good Shepherd,

You died once on the Cross, but you constantly renew your sacrifice through your Church. Each Mass mysteriously renders present your offering on Calvary, your total surrender to the Heavenly Father in a spirit of obedience and love. Its purpose is to enable us to participate in it, so that your sacrifice becomes fully that of the Church.

Help us, through the Mass, to unite our personal offering to the heroic offering you made on Golgotha!

⚜

XIII

☩

JESUS IS TAKEN DOWN FROM THE CROSS

O good Shepherd,

You have ceased to suffer but she who receives your body into her arms, as it is taken down from the Cross, has not yet reached the end of her sorrow. The sword of your death continues to pierce her heart. She prolongs your Passion by her compassion, and she is the image of the Church, who receives your body to perpetuate your sacrifice.

Help us to receive your Eucharistic Body with fervent devotion, so that we may be perfectly united with your redeeming love.

⚜

XIV

✠

JESUS IS LAID
IN THE TOMB

O good Shepherd,

In your burial, your hidden presence in your Church is symbolically prefigured. You wanted to disappear from the eyes of men in order to remain spiritually among them. The life you give to the Church is a hidden life, plunged in the darkness of faith, nourished by an invisible love.

Help us, along with the whole Church, to believe despite the veil of mystery, to hope despite the darkness, to love in silence!

⚜

✠ ✠ ✠ ✠ ✠ ✠ ✠ ✠ ✠ ✠ ✠ ✠ ✠ ✠

7

⚜

A WAY OF THE CROSS
FOR THE SOULS
IN PURGATORY

✠ ✠ ✠ ✠ ✠ ✠ ✠ ✠

I

✠

JESUS IS CONDEMNED TO DEATH

Lord Jesus, sacrificed for our eternal good,

You offered yourself up to death in order to give us life. Deign to grant the fullness of your divine life to the suffering souls in Purgatory!

In memory of your total sacrifice, free them from their sufferings and open to them the door to heavenly blessedness!

⚜

II

✠

JESUS RECEIVES
HIS CROSS

Lord Jesus, sacrificed for our eternal good,

You took up the Cross, in order to alleviate the burdens in our lives weighed down by sin.

Deign to relieve the sufferings of souls who have not yet finished atoning for their sins!

In memory of the weight of your Cross, alleviate their debt and hasten the moment of their deliverance!

⚜

III

✠

JESUS FALLS
THE FIRST TIME

Lord Jesus, sacrificed for our eternal good,

You fell, overwhelmed by the weight of the Cross, in order to free souls overwhelmed by their past. Deign to offer to the souls subject to the torments of Purgatory the freedom you have won for them!

In memory of your first fall, free these souls from the sorrowful consequences of their falls!

⚜

IV

✠

JESUS MEETS
HIS MOTHER

Lord Jesus, sacrificed for our eternal good,

On the way to Calvary, you met your Mother, united with you in your desire to save men and ensure them of eternal blessedness.

Deign now to behold the eyes of your Mother interceding with you for the suffering souls in Purgatory!

In memory of all she suffered in union with you, grant these souls their ultimate good!

⚜

V

✠

SIMON HELPS JESUS TO CARRY HIS CROSS

Lord Jesus, sacrificed for our eternal good,

You associated Simon of Cyrene with your sacrifice. Deign to look at all the souls who, on this earth, want to carry the Cross with you, and allow their generosity to benefit the souls in Purgatory!

In memory of those who agree to accompany you on the road to Calvary, have mercy on these suffering souls!

⚜

VI

✠

VERONICA WIPES
THE FACE OF JESUS

Lord Jesus, sacrificed for our eternal good,

You imprinted your beautiful, loving face on Veronica's cloth.

Deign to admit to the contemplation of your divine face the souls in Purgatory who burn with such an ardent desire to see you!

In memory of all those who are filled with compassion by your sorrowful face, show these souls your glorious face!

⚜

VII

✠

JESUS FALLS
THE SECOND TIME

Lord Jesus, sacrificed for our eternal good,

Your second fall shows how much you suffered, and with what humility.

Deign to allow the souls for whom you offered so much suffering to taste the fruit of it without delay!

In memory of your second fall, erase from the souls in Purgatory the memory of their falls, and give them the joy you have paid for so dearly!

⚜

VIII

✠

JESUS SPEAKS TO THE WOMEN OF JERUSALEM

Lord Jesus, sacrificed for our eternal good,

In the words addressed to the women of Jerusalem, you reveal the compassion in your heart for the suffering of others.

Have compassion on the souls in Purgatory and deign to ease their condition!

In memory of your sympathy for all the unfortunate, show these souls all your mercy!

⚜

IX

✠

JESUS FALLS
THE THIRD TIME

Lord Jesus, sacrificed for our eternal good,

In your third fall, your courage did not weaken because you want to offer everything for souls to be saved.

Deign to procure for the souls in Purgatory the eternal good that your indomitable courage has won for them!

In memory of your third fall and your renewed determination to reach Calvary, allow these souls to hasten on toward you!

⚜

X

☩

JESUS IS STRIPPED
OF HIS GARMENTS

Lord Jesus, sacrificed for our eternal good,

You allowed yourself to be stripped of every-thing so that you can enrich us with the trea-sures of your grace on this earth, and with the treasures of your glory in Heaven.

Deign to lavish at last upon the souls in Pur-gatory the heavenly riches that you have pre-pared for them!

In memory of your complete deprivation, grant these souls the supreme treasure of pos-sessing you yourself!

⚜

XI

☩

JESUS IS NAILED
TO THE CROSS

Lord Jesus, sacrificed for our eternal good,

With heroic patience, you let yourself be nailed to the Cross, and you thereby enabled us to escape the torments deserved by our sins.

Deign to spare the souls in Purgatory any further torments!

In memory of the nails driven into your hands and feet, free these souls from their chains and take them to yourself!

⚜

XII

✠

JESUS DIES ON THE CROSS

Lord Jesus, sacrificed for our eternal good,

You made a wonderful promise to the repentant thief: "Today you will be with me in Paradise" (Lk 23:43).

You, who were so eager to take him to Heaven, deign to hasten to lead the souls in Purgatory there!

In memory of this generous promise, bring them, even today if possible, into paradise!

⚜

XIII

✙

JESUS IS TAKEN DOWN FROM THE CROSS

Lord Jesus, sacrificed for our eternal good,

With what sorrow Mary received your inert and lifeless body!

Since she offered her suffering for the salvation of humanity, deign to allow the souls in Purgatory to benefit from your Mother's sacrifice!

In memory of the sword of sorrow that pierced her maternal heart, grant many of her children the joy of meeting her in Heaven!

⚜

XIV

✠

JESUS IS LAID
IN THE TOMB

Lord Jesus, sacrificed for our eternal good,

The stone that closed your tomb could not imprison you there; your sepulcher opened and you came forth triumphant.

Deign to associate the souls of Purgatory with your triumph!

In memory of the tomb you opened, open wide the gates of deliverance to them and grant them access to their heavenly home!

⚜

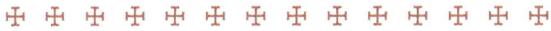

✠ ✠ ✠ ✠ ✠ ✠ ✠ ✠ ✠ ✠ ✠ ✠ ✠

APPENDIX

⚜

A PICTORIAL
WAY OF THE CROSS

Paintings by
Caryll Houselander

✠ ✠ ✠ ✠ ✠ ✠ ✠ ✠

I

✠

JESUS IS CONDEMNED TO DEATH

⚜

II

✠

JESUS RECEIVES
HIS CROSS

⚜

III

✠

JESUS FALLS
THE FIRST TIME

⚜

IV

☩

JESUS MEETS HIS MOTHER

V

SIMON HELPS JESUS
TO CARRY HIS CROSS

⚜

VI

✠

VERONICA WIPES
THE FACE OF JESUS

⚜

VII

✠

JESUS FALLS
THE SECOND TIME

VIII

✠

JESUS SPEAKS TO THE WOMEN OF JERUSALEM

IX

✠

JESUS FALLS
THE THIRD TIME

⚜

X

✠

JESUS IS STRIPPED OF HIS GARMENTS

⚜

XI

✠

JESUS IS NAILED TO THE CROSS

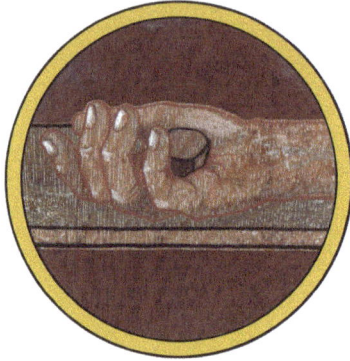

⚜

XII

✠

JESUS DIES ON THE CROSS

⚜

XIII

JESUS IS TAKEN DOWN
FROM THE CROSS

XIV

✠

JESUS IS LAID
IN THE TOMB

⚜

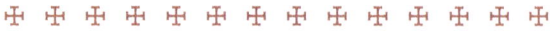

Scimus Christum surrexisse a mortuis vere:
tu nobis, victor Rex, miserere.

We know that Christ has truly risen from the dead.
O, victorious King, have mercy on us.
(THE EASTER SEQUENCE)

128

www.ingramcontent.com/pod-product-compliance
Lightning Source LLC
Chambersburg PA
CBHW050818090426
42737CB00021B/3431